A Coral Reef

Julie Haydon

Rigby

This is a coral reef.

Coral reefs are found in warm sea water.

Coral looks like a plant, but it is really an animal.

5

Coral is a strange animal, because it cannot move around.

It uses its tentacles to catch food.

7

A coral reef can take thousands of years to form.

Some coral reefs are so big they can be seen from space!

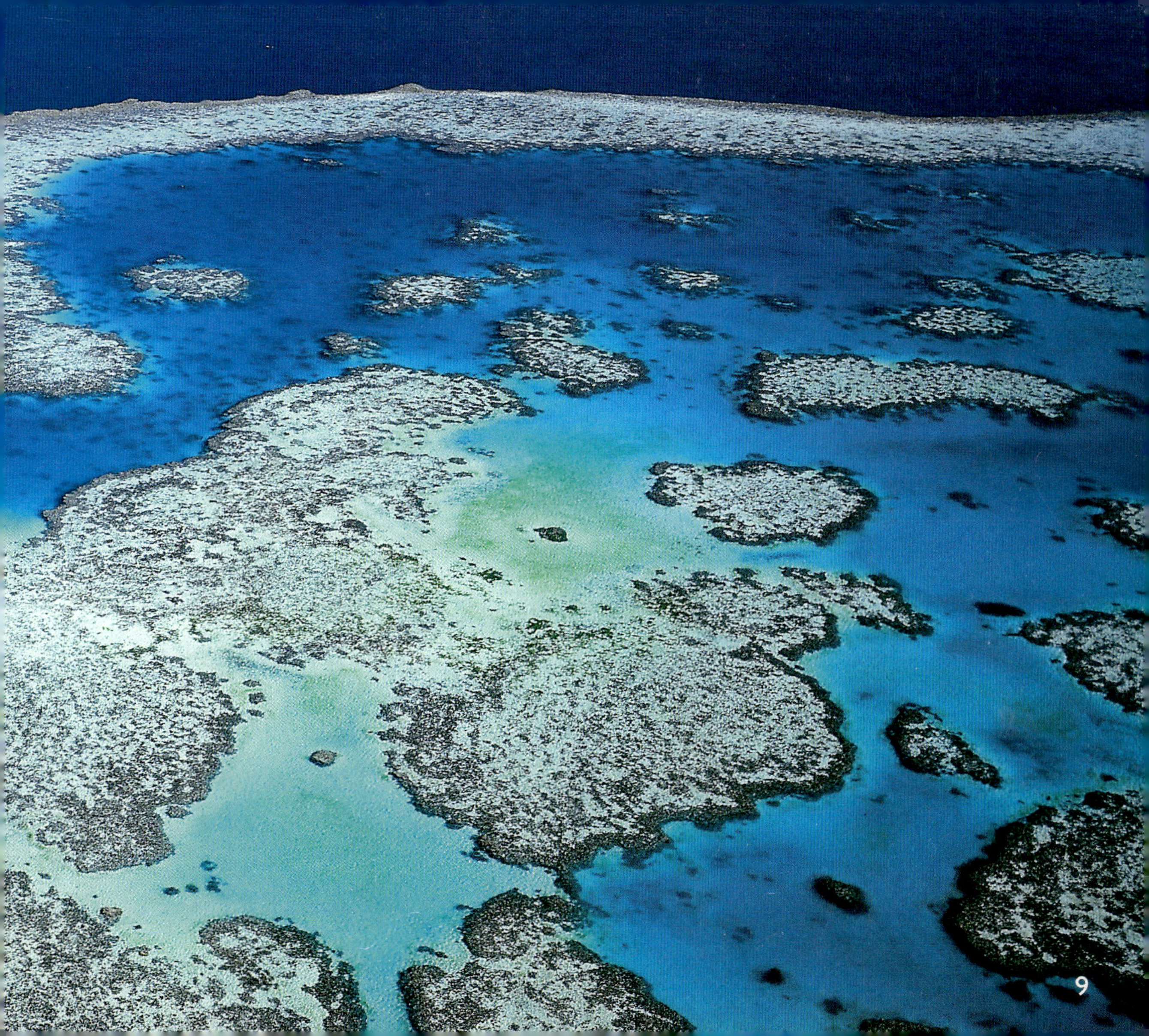

Many sea animals live in a coral reef.

This seahorse lives in a coral reef.

A seahorse changes color to hide in the coral.

This starfish lives in a coral reef.

A starfish eats clams and oysters.

This parrotfish lives in a coral reef.

A parrotfish eats tiny plants that grow on the coral.

This hermit crab lives in a coral reef.

A hermit crab uses a shell as a home.

This octopus lives in a coral reef.

An octopus has eight tentacles to help it swim and catch food.

True or false?

Coral reefs:

1 are found in cold sea water.

2 are full of sea animals.

3 can be big.

4 take only a few years to form.

Answers : 1 false 2 true 3 true 4 false